Last Night I Aged a Hundred Years

Last Night I Aged a Hundred Years

poems

Peter Grandbois

Winner of the 2020 Richard Snyder Publication Prize
Selected by Indran Amirthanayagam

The Ashland Poetry Press

Printed in the United States of America
ISBN: 978-0-912592-93-0
Library of Congress Card Catalogue Number: 2021930578

Author photo: Tanya Wilson
Cover art: Tommy White; reproduced by permission
Cover design: Nicholas Fedorchak
Book layout: Mark E. Cull
Editing: Jennifer Rathbun and Deborah Fleming

Acknowledgments

After the Pause: "Silence"; "Tell me how to speak"

Atlanta Review: "Another rainy morning in Ohio"; "Sometimes at night"

DIALOGIST: "Ask me"

The Gettysburg Review: "Dusk"

Hiram Poetry Review: "Wondering which names to sing"

Jelly Bucket: "The kiss"; "When does the moon"

Kettle Blue Review: "I thought I would still my body"

Lake Effect: "Because a bird"

Louisiana Literature: "This is not a dream"

The Madison Review: "We are the ones"

The Meadow: "The dog was not put down"; "Burning"; "The blue door"

Mercury: "This shuffling across"; "Who is remember me"

North Dakota Quarterly: "There is no beyond"; "This poem is not"; "I am your silence"

Poetry South: "There is nowhere to begin"

The Potomac Review: "The inconsolable wind"; "Poking through the void"

Prism Review: "Last night I aged a hundred years"; "So small this word, a cloud"; "Where even the wind"

The Summerset Review: "What gravity wants"

Sweet Tree Review: "Weather"

Timberline Review: "There is a mouth that speaks before it stutters"

Turtle Island Quarterly: "When I was alive"

Typehouse: "The cup we share"

Verdad: "Drowning"; "Sometimes we are so close"

Contents

III

They that are awake have one world in common, but of the sleeping each turns aside into a world of his own.

—*Heraclitus*

True music is the music of silence, the silent but well-heard music of thought in the head, passion in the body, reverie in the soul.

—*Juan Ramón Jiménez*

Dusk

I found my body outside,

lying along the edge of the road

one evening like an open

palm,

water whispering through

a seam

of earth like a thread I might

follow,

stories spinning overhead, a drift

of stars

speaking pools of brackish

grief

only a fool wouldn't believe.

This world is never fully

ours.

I placed a hand upon its chest,

tried to feel the lift

and fall,

when from somewhere beyond

this shawl

of sleep,

a crow took

flight.

Or maybe I was the crow,

and the thing at the edge of the road

a darkening house I watched, waiting

for the last light to go out.

There is nowhere to begin

Except in snow
stretching across a field
in late March,

A crow in the branches
standing against
the long riffs of wind.

In a few weeks' time
the rapture of alder, ash, and elm,

the almost forgetting of Galanthus
bloom

and hawks
soaring with sun-forged feathers,

mapping the secrets
of the invisible world—

Why are we always
leaving,
or being left?

And how do we clear away
this winter we carry

inside?

❧

Today, for example, I was thinking
                                    that I wasn't
                                                anyone,

that I don't know when it's time to stop
                                                pretending.

❧

The calculus of light
                        that holds us
                                                keeps shifting,

even the fox standing wary
                                    at the edge
                                                of the clearing,

or the squirrel dancing
                                    around that tree,
                                                gathering what little it can,

are no longer the same.

❧

We move so
            slowly,

Like steam
rising over the high grass,

waiting to see what face
we'll turn toward
home.

A complete and perfect silence

I woke this morning
thinking I was a bird
but I was simply old

I walked to breakfast
carrying an ocean
but it was only
the prayers of the faithful

Regret is like snow—
it falls until we
are emptied of words

Better to touch
                your hand
Better to bleed
                in your house
Better to let
                the lice suck
A new stitching
                in the sky

When the darkness comes
I'd like a map to tell me
exactly where to stand

Because a bird

I refuse to exist inside this body's
hard equation, the stippled exhalation
of days that begin because a bird
imagined morning as a house of flowers
with pale skin, and, dressing itself in yellows
and reds, sang through this tangle of brutal
longing into all we can't understand,
like the connection between yesterday,
when I knew how to remember,
tomorrow, where I am the crossroads
between barren breath and surfeit of sun,
and today, a line drawn from eye to hand,
an intimate knock at the throated door
from a stranger who doesn't want to come in.

Let's begin with what we cannot hear

The sleeper's dream wrapped in stone

The whisper of web the spider floats upon

Long-fingered sunlight
across the rain-soaked street

Swollen red leaves the moment
you speak

The light at the center of the twig
your dog carries
in its mouth

The ceremony of darkness in the box
of your cardboard childhood

The warm baritone of the lone pine
singing at the field's edge
at dusk

The forgotten
road

The buzz and clamor of growing
old

Sometimes we are so close

Sometimes we are so close
to the god-throat
of nothing

The sky empties us
and we enter the room
left behind

Roam the blue absence
between tell me another lie
and don't speak

If you look deep enough
even darkness
has a shadow

Watch the way it threads itself
through secrets
and stone,

Connecting every sleeper
to another
ocean

The water laps against the sand
and we open
into many

Nothing ends here

Sometimes I live in a small sound
of waiting,

of a light we can never quite have,

or of ghosts haunting
a departed garden

And time and memory seem bound
to the visible
world

as I step down through eyes
of birds,

the knotted crown that separates before
and after

No edges No ties
Only the fatal sheen of leaves
after rain,

a thread stitched through
the flesh

of losses we dare not claim

moving us far from all we are
to nothing
/ends here/

to there is always another
night
lying just beyond
this body

Sometimes I cease to be the spider

Hanging against this pale ceilinged sky

On those nights no border will help me

And silence multiplies until nothing is

Recognizable, until I can't

Remember the flies hanging

In the far corners of my web

If I remember at all, it's more like

The fluttering wings of a ghost self—

The doors of the blind open both ways

And we who cry the terrible drift

Of our desire at two in the morning

Are only several thousand threads

And four hours short of the inexpertly

Drawn and frenzied state of every god

We wanted to be

Housekeeping

We have been cleaning for days

You know

As if the world were still a place
that could be imagined

And childhood a day in which
we believed

We have been cleaning for weeks

You know

As if we could live somewhere
solid

And the terrible thing inside
was nothing but a gesture
toward laughter

We have been cleaning for months

You know

As if dust could disguise
a body

like snow covering a tree

We have been cleaning for years

You know

As if the home
we were making
was a kind of eye

that wanted
to be seen

This shuffling across

My fingers stretch like ghosts
all night
in the quavering snow,
cold

seeping through my coat
like a memory or a mouth
too full

to contain anything but tentacles
of breath

as if my wandering could lead
to this lake
(door once opened)

that lies between moonlight
and silence,

between the swelling of trees
and what can be gathered
by wind

as if there were a word for the
flickering

eyes of stars

this shuffling

across snarled shadows of sleeping
pines

this music

that sings of stumbling

in the dark and the endless

burden of /being /

/knowing/

/nothing/ is there

When does the moon

turn away   ashamed   and when does it decide

to pour into   a body   or whatever

cathedral   it claims   for its own

Flower moon   Blood moon   Harvest moon   Hunter's moon

Some names keep   better   the more   shadows

we wrap   about us   And why can't we   spin too

like a drunk   searching for a new   face

in night's   barking thrum   or sometimes

mistake   sunrise   for sunset   as if

we weren't stuck   in the thinnest of days

Strawberry moon   Pink moon   Blue moon   Super moon

What is it about   the creatures   we already know

why they prefer   to scurry   along the far side

of our hungry brains   where not even the stars

remember   how to fold back   into light

So small this word, a cloud

So small this word, a cloud.
So light this tiny curl
of flesh, so bright this day
as yet unexploded.

And sometimes just a match
is enough.

And sometimes when I'm still
the spark goes out,

as if the pink mouthed afternoons
weren't insistent,

as if these comings
and goings
could happen
to anyone else—

in this we are mistaken.

There is a mouth that speaks before it stutters

I've been trying to tell you
                                        I am not
what happened
to me

not
this flock of hands
cutting through blue
night
like the ghosts
you want
             to see

Because the desire to create
and destroy
are equal
I wake
to find black stones
in my mouth
my tongue
a half step closer
to god

Because it takes distance
to understand
you walk
between the two
worlds
until we

are a song
becoming
a memory
of fire
until we
are empty
enough

We know how this ends

We have already undressed

We want this
to be easy

The kiss

What you see is not
your life
opening
like a moth
when you look in the mirror

more like a crow flying
sideways
as if to better know
the night

And the white stutter
of sleep
moves like a swarm
of scissors
cutting through your head,
reminding you
some things always return

like the dream and drift
of minor gods

Don't sit and spend the day
suspicious
of beginnings
in this house of broken
windows
until darkness returns
like a kiss
filled with trembling
answers
a hole torn
in a veil

Who is remember me

If only I could lose the small in me
The way birds remember sky in wind's embrace,

Or a ship's oars stretch as the sea veil lifts,
The whale's shadow deepening the wine-dark,

Or the way I soared over the trees
Having hit the jump on my sled just right.

My twelve-year-old friends below diminished
As my body song extended in flight,

Head tilted back, arms outspread, rowing toward
The murmur of mouth spilled open to madness,

Or something like it, assuming nothing
But the sweep, the soft-stroked weep of being.

What remains hidden

Begin with the night
and the fact that flesh
is not completely
star-grown
or choose the morning
that lies to you
about your puzzle
of unstated need.
It doesn't matter
which story you pluck
from your wind-blown pain
it's all been paid for—
this brief dialogue
between blood and bone.
You become one thing
and then another,
trying to keep hidden,
to keep from being
swept into unknown,
when all you need do
is take into
your body all things,
accept that all things
move toward moan.

II

The dog was not put down

Sometimes I sleep and then this dream
Where I'm trying to talk to you

After years of not

In this version, we're standing in a soft forest,
The secret of snow shivering about us

And when my hands
Held the box with his ashes

And the receptionist asked if
He'd been euthanized—she'd needed
To know for the final bill—I said

The dog was not put down.

We're cracking as we walk
Across the December cold,
Small fissures rising through us—

A hawk circling above the pines,
Like a vision of who
We really are—

I want to speak
To say something
Before the dream ends

I open my mouth
But catch only snow

❧

This morning I sit in my chair
All tangled in being alive,
The box behind me on the shelf

And I'm thinking of your last breath
How you stood and stared past me
Your mouth open

How it seemed as if you wanted
To give me   something

❧

Who among us hasn't wished to leave
our bodies

To spread ourselves
In the wild woods
Behind the back fence

And wait for the right name to come

Drowning

The spirit lives between
one name and another

Between the silences we let slip
and the tiny aches we hold onto

Between the head tilted back
and the mouth left open to rain

This morning I woke under the kitchen table
looking for my shadow

I mean my dog, Shadow

I mopped the floor where he spent his last night
Then tried to vacuum the stray hairs

As if death was a place you could clean

As if we weren't all, always, waiting
for our next face

To come true

But the floor wouldn't dry
So the hairs stuck to the wall, the vacuum,
everything

Let us walk to the river and find a new
god

one with slippery green skin
to let the water in

We are the ones

Having spent the night tending my dog

diminishing into his own forest

of silence I'd thought there was something

to fear in the dark some bridge we weren't

supposed to cross like the sky even

the river is tired the body pushes

toward prayer I'd thought there was a morning

to be relieved but we are the ones

who dissolve into breath from moon to mouth

we cannot count How do we open

to death If I were awake I could

mop all the water that seeps from him

We try to find small comforts for each other

to be that part the other has forgotten

I'd thought there were so many words to say

but I have been careless and now there is

only his throat sounding   the one question

I   can't   answer

I thought I would still my body

I mean cease to feel

The way my dog hid

Beneath the wheelbarrow

On his last day

❧

I thought I would see you in my dreams

I mean a finger

Touched to a mouth

Staked in that hard place

❧

I thought I would call my father

More often

I mean that underneath each word

Is a window

Scratched into a wall

❧

I remember as a child walking alone

Down the dark reservoir spillway

I mean the mud-filled sewer beneath my street

I mean depression

I remember running through school

To throw up in the bathroom

So no one could see

I mean I found my dog beneath the wheelbarrow.

I remember flying.

I remember hitting the jump with our sled too fast

Soaring over the tops of snow-dusted trees.

Then, I remember nothing, except that

Because we were flying

We never needed to turn away.

A boy woke one morning with night sweats

Last night in the dark
I woke drenched in sweat,
an envoy from another world,
born into this cave of night,
and I swore I could see you
standing across the bulging
neck of time, fourteen,
a face unfettered by webs,
all your desires still intact,
and I wondered what,
if anything, we had
to talk about, what warning
could I give about the ways
in which the emptiness
calls us to fill our days?

I suspect you knew
this already, or else
why visit at all, why
stand there patiently
waiting for me to wake,
to sip the cold tea
beside my bed until
you open your mouth
sounding as if you're
underwater, while I'm
the one who is drowning.

And then it's me standing
on the other side, looking
at the figure in the bed.
I want to tell him everything,
that this world is an ocean

that fills your head
with words darker than oil,
that every premonition
is little better than borrowed
breath, that most of what
we see merely skates
the dim surface of desire.

Instead, when he wakes
and looks at me with
eyes that spill into
every false path home,
I imagine us walking
together to the life
neither of us will see.
So much beauty gone
So much yet to come.

Forget the prayers

you learned in childhood, the "Our Fathers" and "Hail Mary's" you
whispered while crossing yourself in bed at night, adding at the end how
you'd recite ten more if only your teacher would die, the test postponed.
Forget the times you pretended to cry so you wouldn't have to go to church.
Forget the rabbit's foot and lucky shirt. Or the ways you folded yourself into
a TV corner to forget the lie of each passing day. Forget sage. Forget amulets,
crosses, and ankhs. Four-leaf clovers and horseshoes. It's been several nights
of crowed sleep, dreams filled with the cloved breath of ghosts and houses
with shuttered windows, scythes swinging before locked and bleeding rows
of doors. And no pillow over your head, no covers pulled to your chin can
shield you from the sight of your tumored life stabbed to the bedroom floor.
No shot of whiskey, no poetry read to fool you into falling line by line into
that cold country of choler and bone can keep you from the dark laughter
that calls like the siren's wind-blown song to the shadowy figure crouched in
the corner with the knife, a face strangely like your own.

This is not a dream

Sometimes I think I see an open mouth
breathing secrets like autumn leaves,

other times a face that speaks sorrow like crows
spreading their dark wings in winter's first light.

And sometimes I am so ashamed I sit
far away from human sounds, like a frog

scavenging through a meditation of mud,
other times, I lie in bed late at night

when the hours transform each noise to blood,
thinking I've slipped free of this dreamed skin,

and I listen once more to the din of crickets
trembling through my bedroom window,

their riddled song a hand on my chest I must
divine. Or am I lying on the floor,

or sitting there in the corner, legs crossed,
the open mouth nothing more than a hole,

and there I am again at the back of it.

Another rainy morning in Ohio

And I'm thinking about my childhood
In Denver. I must have been thirteen
Or fourteen. No matter. It's November
And the wind's slow, cold breath
Rimes the branches of every tree,
And a covenant of blood-red leaves
Cling to the Japanese Maple
In our front yard, and I stand before it
Basking in the amniotic light
Gathering, like loneliness, in the shards,
Until my father calls me to join him.
He says he needs me for an errand,
That we'll return soon and then I can play.
What he doesn't say is that we'll be
Breaking and entering, stealing a console
TV he can't lift himself from renters
who are behind on their rent.
I'll never forget the fear limning his mouth
When he told me to hurry up as I strained
Under the load, how he reminded me
They could return any minute, that they
Wouldn't take kindly to finding us
In the middle of their living room.
That night, I lie in bed watching the moon
Slipping loose from the winter sky,
Just as now, in the absence of the present,
I find myself raking wet leaves into
The forest at the edge of our yard,
Wondering how this song of praise
Became a confession of crows, wishing
That this time the cold would descend
Like the original blood of the world
And that ice would rime the branches once again.

Ask me

why   my father   held out   his hands   when I threw up   in the

hospital hallway   at age five   and I will tell   you   there are

many   unplanned ways   to say   I am   the color   of trees

and even   in error the body   speaks rain   Ask   why   my

father was   in such a hurry   to hang up   today   and I will tell

you   it's better to   fasten   yourself   to this   tiny   leaf

of a world   than   to   wander   avenues   of regret

Remember   the high   oaks   the   sycamores   and   white birch

they   are   your loves   given   back   to you   as if   you could   pass

through   days of   sickness   and   walk   once   again

into   the church   of those   hands

I am your silence

Let the blood's dim dance lead us through
whatever childhood we are resisting.
Let the body's tender tilt take us
tumbling past the dark nest of endless
mouths to each and every outcast name
shoved to the dirt. Something I heard today
reminded me of this poem, something
in the trembling forest of your voice
and the backward slant of your cantering
throat. Let's say I need you to breathe—
let's pretend it's that simple.

The inconsolable wind

Sometimes I'm ashamed of the frost
that silvers the grass each morning,
so obvious in its need to conceal.
Or the slow unraveling of moon-bathed
night that trembles to reveal
a kingdom where sight no longer
rules—and the red-eyed raccoons,
and the cries of loons, and the dogs
howling at the—no, not the moon—
at each other. That's really what
this is about, isn't it? The need to cross
between, the mornings we sip tea
made in a far-off country wondering
at every fifteen-cent life left unseen.

Weather

And there are days when the body expects
to usurp the flock of starlings winging
against the squirm of mid-morning cold.

And others when the mind breathes its own dust,
like an asthmatic city choking on
the moldy gasp of autumn's failing light.

And those when our voices wake to find
they have no more claim on us than an ocean
curling toward the delightful shape of shore.

And so what is left to do but tender
the field between hip and thigh, fold
our wrinkled past about us like a pressed

shirt, undressing regret until each
cloud reflects an empty sky.

Poking through the void

How can we believe the water
strider when starlings circle
above the shimmering glass,
or the hare's hunger when
the white owl spreads its wings?
How do we know if we are the dog's
dream or simply a shadow in it?
We will our house toward prayer
when our wanderings should become
our words. We climb the staircase
toward the far field when the lone
sapling that watched over us stands
near. The hour moves, filled with breath
and marrow, and the world ends here

Though it is dark now my grief

Though it is dark now my grief

sparrows into light

Collapsing day

into your long arms

An uneasy field un-

folding soft rapture

Can you hold it still

as the sky erases the stars

Sometimes a body

contains more sound

Than body

Silence

What happens first and then
snow? What ends and then
the smell of bright dust?
An hour before the birds
and then maybe no one
can remember. A moment
after the stray tangle
of twilight and then
the dog panting and
shifting on the rug—
maybe it's like that.

III

Instruction manual for growing old

Don't believe you are this thing
you have become

When the late wasps
return home

And all that snow
like people falls

Through this temporary
world

❧

Don't assume the voices
of distant memories
are your own

Or that this library of the soul
is made only of books
recently on loan

❧

Hold fast to plans
when another windblown
god flies through the room

And step first into darkness
when returning home

❧

Know that when you sleep
you are someone else

And that the clock face
at four a.m.

Is a riddle you need not decipher

Know, too, that to speak
the name of your beloved
Is to make a fist of bees

And this is just one of the ways
to be deceived

Such as every moment
you believe

That to be trapped
in this body

Means only to hear
the haunted

Walking round and round
the basement laundry

Searching for light
in the sound of rain

As if they could touch
    that fractured sky again

❧

Open your hands
    to the ordinary corners

And call each distant
    particle of evening

By its true name

Where even the wind

What voice will take you
        Where evening sings
Where even the wind
        Wanders lost

What song will lead
        Where oceans sleep
And hours rain
        On starving skin

This place we call home
        Mistakes us for bodies
When we are dreams
        Of light

Enraged by flocks
        Of black birds
Mouths severed
        By stars

Let us drink
        To the jagged gods
Of darkness
        Taking shape inside

Imagine unknotting
        The owl's breath
That binds us
        To longing

Make your way
    Through the frozen field
Come on
    Slip off your shoes

Fold your clothes
    Into gratitude
Take the first step
    We're waiting

This poem is not

Once I moved to a condo

beside a graveyard.

Each night I stood

on the balcony

naked in the dusk,

staring at headstones,

the light wrapping

about me

like a river,

or a blanket

of grief

kept in a secret

room,

until I ran

out
of memory,

until there was

no difference

between

what I saw

and what

I conjured

from the mud.

This poem is not

necessary,

not anything like

the calligraphy of snow,

the dancing of barren

branches

in the wind,

an occultation

above our heads.

It is not

a revelation

from an ancient world

or another way

across the river

unless

that is exactly

what you need.

Sometimes at night

I feel my body
deepening to trees,
trickling into
pools that whisper
like the eyes of birds.
And memory
like a spidery
beard grows thick,
pulling me through
one door and into
another where I
open my hands
to the darkness
before me but cup
only the owl's cry
drawn from this
unwieldy air.

Where are the fields
with their honeyed
light? Where the
scalloped moon?
Where the fluttering
sleep that slips beyond
this muffled meaning?
Where the parade
of stars that might lead
back to the fabric
of day, that pale
and unfinished dream?

In the morning,
when fog enshrouds you

like a cloak, don't
be afraid to glance,
just once, behind you,
to listen to
altars built by
turning away.
There are voices
in the river.

Wondering which names to sing

Sometimes I am so small
I fasten myself to crickets
Other times the geese curve
Around my horizon

Some mornings I am more memory
Than person and can only hope
To find my body within the pines
Beyond my back yard

There are days when I am
A tiny seizure of joy
And others when I resist kneeling
Before the loom of mid-afternoon light

It's never too late to become
The low cloud carried to dark, to hear
The voices outside the cell
Of your cauterized fear

To wake each morning is to break
Into the wounded fragrance of bees,
The fluttering feathers of leaves,
Invisible threads unstitching the world

Tell me how to speak

Of beginnings
of prairies deep
as oceans and
darkness bound
by flame

Tell me how to leave
in pieces
the softest parts
of us, or how
to convince the trees
to reveal their secret
cathedral

When sometimes silence
licks the night,
until endings
hit like a lover's
backward glance,

and we're left
standing beneath
a stunted sky,
arms upraised,
shuddering
before our own
nakedness

There is no beyond

Say you find yourself in a wilderness
following the many names of dusk
like windows into alluvial night.

Say that behind each dream is another,
conjuring the past like a sepulchral
shroud through which we stutter our way,

or that the cold-stoked flames of autumn leaves
are nothing more than a thousand little doors
opening like mouths dying to speak.

Today, like every other day, I read
of violence in the field, news on my phone
washing over me in waves of blood.

And still horizons call in widening
spirals of abject silence, a reminder
that what we have forgotten frees us

And still a conspiracy of ravens—
those keepers of ancient longings—
gathers in the forest's heart, a token

of that part of ourselves that never sleeps,
the hidden perfection of moonlight on bone.

Lying down to die in a field in Paxton, Massachusetts

I dream myself a new song
From the bile in my mouth,
One where my ghost does not
Follow me from town to town,
Rest stop to rest stop like a plague
Or a bad stomach bug.
Lost midway along the journey
To the hotel I called home
When winter was my midwife.
Now the wind blows through my hair
And I close the car doors
Like a madman's coat and
Listen to the moths beating
On the window while I summon
All the workings of letting go
Because I refuse to exist
Without mystery.
I lean the car seat back,
Uncoiling all I've been
Or will ever be, and watch
The roof of the car haloed
In silver lakes of moonlight.
It seems I'm the last to know
There's a trembling inside
Stillness, and nothing solid
Is really solid, and this tiny,
Bleeding world is beautiful
Beyond understanding.
My dear friend, do you see all
I am saying? Do you hear
Each of your heartbeats,
Fruit made of summer's light?

Last night I aged a hundred years

Last night I aged a hundred years
As if a downdraft of birds

This morning, at breakfast the locusts came
As if this small rain weren't enough

I fear the afternoon will refuse me
As if the ladder could stand against the house

Now I cannot sing, or will not
As if the field inside were clear

And hunchbacked day won't come again
And how to lie awake in disapproving

Silence and not feel the hours of torn
And how close can two worlds get anyway

The scribbled edges of one body scratching
Against another, as if the next wound

Hadn't already happened, as if the
Riddled mouth would not cry this dream again.

Sometimes I say what I don't want

Then weave myself a song that sounds

Like stars wheeling in a field

Where skin dreams an echo of fingers

Moving through black birds of hair.

Other times I am a seam of silt

Edging a hole filled with words

No one dares hear—ghosted foam

At the ocean's moon-dark edge

Where the ballad of blood begs

The body's forgiveness and maybe

We catch a glimpse of ourselves and

This is why people need other people to hold them.

The mud-riddled song of morning

Breaks us
same as the pull of missing
                                        names
at noon

And the untranslatable
borders   of lovers
          that line
the evening

And still we rise
                              each day
from dreams that tend
                              toward fatuous sky
speaking words
          that fall like blows
telling stories
          we thought would lead
where we wanted
          to go

How have we come
all this way
          only to remain
strangers

I can't help wonder
how   we   might   touch

each other
as if we wanted
to know

What gravity wants

is for the slow burn
       of childhood
              to end,
for the long day
       to bend
          toward emptiness,
What wind wants
       is forgetting,
              to rend past from flesh—
was that us, there,
       waving on the bridge in the snow,
or there, tending
       to the dogs as they play in the field—
until this body
       is no longer
              our home.
But remember—
       everything depends
              on this one small thing—
we carry within
       the seed of our own
              beginning,
and something new is written
              the moment we surrender
to sky.
    This loop of being,
              this stillness between—
sometimes it blooms.

The blue door

We are only October's
Dream drifting fog down
The forest path where
The slender spider
Like whispering hands
Ballets the quiet,
Only a woven coat
Biting back omens
Of emptiness and cold
That gutter alleys and
Throats choked with rain,
Only a revenant
With eyes closed
To former selves and
Winds that shape them
Into thin notes that
Crack and snap like
Bewitched twigs beneath
Bleeding feet shuffling
Through their own
Schizophrenic syntax
Of desire that threads
Through our bodies
Until with lanterns
Lit like open hands
We step into ghosts
Stitched from all we are
Or have ever been,
Into the fire burning
Into the church of stone
Into the blue bird
Singing the only door

That leads to the only
Sky we might call home.

Burning

Ask me why this body
        That is everywhere

Or why all the river wants
        Is forgiveness

Ask why the scars you can't see
        Or why I am a pouring

Of trees that fall toward silence
        Ask why we need

Claw back to the wild
        Like raccoons in the night

When even the blind know
        The sentences that break

Like shards are not the song
        But only a way to remember

And words that fall
        From trembling mouths

Are nothing but a false stillness
        That slips about us like fog

When we are the lanterns

The cup we share

Where is the map to the next world
That country of stray dogs

Where everything I have to say
I can say in the dark

And the cup we share
Is a house

Small enough to fit
Under the pillow

And the time that lies
Between us

Folds smaller
And smaller

Until the air unwinds
And we wake

To the steeper path
Of sorrow

You know the one
The ghost-covered stair

That trembles through
the sun's slow course

We are always escaping

Ten versions of a life

1.
Sometimes I sit for hours
dreaming of crows.

2.
There are days when the snow
turns everything into some other thing.

3.
I want to ask them, the crows I mean,
what they've left behind.

4.
I wait for them to color me—
black feathers, midnight eyes—
but a hare runs circles in the
drifts, distracting them.

5.
They bob their heads and stretch
their necks, telling stories they don't
believe, or is that their way of listening?

6.
Who can tell what shape
the voice of God might take?

7.
I stand with them, a murder
in the snow, tearing
at some small dead thing,
trying to recall what
I'd meant to do.

8.
Between the crows and
the body of the woman
I love lie so many
hazy days it's difficult
to see the field.

9.
I practice and practice but
how can I be more than my skin?

10.
I have seen a light in the distance.
It is guarded by crows.
Nothing has changed.

When I was alive

I swam the waters of the Cherry Creek,
a catfish trailing a pack of boys armed
with bows and arrows, invisible dusk
descending with the birds and their shadows.

When the first arrow hit, they surrounded
me, too stunned to speak, watching my mouth
open and close, the only answer to fire
silence upon silence into my shining body.

Then there was the time I was a trout
racing down the Platte until a rock
hit me in the back. I watched from the shore
with glassy eyes, morning steam rising

off the river like the voices of the boys
as they argued over who would make
the final blow, as if a stone to the head
could end this unbearable longing.

I suppose it's death I'm talking about.
How our handsewn ghost is always moving
among the haunted, the way last night
I was an injured bird in my friend's backyard,

or how the week before my six legs tried
to scuttle off the Black Cat beneath me,
its fuse counting the seconds until I
was blown across the Colorado field.

How do we open to all we've seen,
all we're told to see, to the tortured hand
of every word we tried to write,
to the catfish head whacked against the rock.

The days are more than we are. We'll never
understand what time makes of us, or when
it's time to drop the oars, let the boat drift,
to be born again beneath a liquid sky.

What we do not sing

You were born in the stillness
between elms and
like branches you were raised
on creak and moan

❧

Five years old and you can't imagine
why there are days without snow
days when the need for another
language can overwhelm

❧

Eleven and what you do not sing
already a circle feeding on itself
like the bullsnake you grabbed by the tail
hoping to keep it from its home

❧

Fourteen and you enter your own whale
crawling the sewer beneath the field
toward old toward groan toward "O
what a dank and sorrowful realm"

❧

At sixteen you wear the crow of silence
like a shield its wings trapping you
in the center of your friends
as if we belonged to ourselves

At twenty-one you search for a doorway
into the body no matter the mouth
mapping the way as you walk only
to find you carried the emptiness within

Thirty-seven and you are born each time
the voice calls you to a house of words
a day made of sand from the other shore
It scares you that the voice is not your own

Forty-seven and the language of you
disappears like a brown bat chasing
an echo into the red river's roar
the nettle's bloom the only clue

Fifty-four and you've slept forever
on a bed of roots where memory
bleeds to black dreaming of your house
but it is here inside this poem

Of what lies beyond, we know nothing
except how the body lies holy
except how what we do not sing clothes us

in light
except how the dazzle of wings within us
might survive

In *Last Night I Aged a Hundred Years* the poet speared this reader early, turning my insides out on the petri dish as he declared at the end of the first poem that he is "waiting to see what face/we'll turn toward/home." The skewering of perspective, the slant light, in the phrase is one of many throughout this luminous collection where light is refracted on a surface of absence, the water never the same when you step in the river for the second time, "when from somewhere beyond/this shawl/of sleep that slips about us each night,/ A sorcerer crow took/flight."

The sorcerer crow is magic, death, a scavenger, a necessary part of the cycle of restitution to earth of what it has produced, this life, this poetry book where one can read life's deep background story. "I woke this morning/thinking I was a bird/but I was simply old . . . I walked to breakfast/carrying an ocean . . . When the darkness comes/I'd like a map to tell me/exactly where to stand."

This book is that map. I know where I stand on earth, in my dreams, as I fly with the crow surveying the land for carrion. I know where I stand as I sway to the death march "the warm baritone of the lone pine/singing at the field's edge/at dusk." And sometimes that standing terrifies "sometimes we are so close/to the god-throat/of nothing. . . . the sky empties us/and we enter the room/left behind . . . roam the blue absence/between tell me another lie/and don't speak."

But at least we know, the poet says, "that nothing ends here . . . there is always another/night/lying just beyond/this body."

Thank you, poet, for allowing me to become a crow, for changing my face and view as I face the road home after I step out abroad for my evening walk. Thank you for the sounds of silence and for the lyric insight "we have been cleaning for days . . . You know . . . As if the world were still a place/that could be imagined/And childhood a day in which/we believed./ We have been cleaning for weeks/ You know/ As if we could live somewhere/solid/ And the terrible thing inside/was nothing but a gesture/toward laughter . . . We have been cleaning for months/ You know . . . . As if the home/we were making/was a kind of eye/ that wanted to be seen."

Thank you for allowing us to see with your homing eye, to age one hundred years in a night of reading, of flying with the crow.

Congratulations for the Snyder Prize waiting for you when you get back home.

Indran Amirthanayagam
Author of *The Migrant States*
Editor of *Beltway Poetry Quarterly*
2020 Snyder Prize Judge

The Richard Snyder Publication Series

This book is the 24th in a series honoring the memory of Richard Snyder (1925–1986), poet, fiction writer, playwright, and longtime professor of English at Ashland University. Snyder served for fifteen years as English Department chair and was co-founder (in 1969) and co-editor of the Ashland Poetry Press. In selecting the manuscript for this book, the editors honor Snyder's tenacious dedication to craftsmanship and thematic integrity.

Deborah Fleming, director and series editor, selected finalists for the 2020 contest.

Final judge was Indran Amirthanayagam.

Snyder Award Winners:

1997: Wendy Battin for *Little Apocalypse*
1998: David Ray for *Demons in the Diner*
1999: Philip Brady for *Weal*
2000: Jan Lee Ande for *Instructions for Walking on Water*
2001: Corrinne Clegg Hales for *Separate Escapes*
2002: Carol Barrett for *Calling in the Bones*
2003: Vern Rutsala for *The Moment's Equation*
2004: Christine Gelineau for *Remorseless Loyalty*
2005: Benjamin S. Grossberg for *Underwater Lengths in a Single Breath*
2006: Lorna Knowles Blake for *Permanent Address*
2007: Helen Pruitt Wallace for *Shimming the Glass House*
2008: Marc J. Sheehan for *Vengeful Hymns*
2009: Jason Schneiderman for *Striking Surface*
2010: Mary Makofsky for *Traction*
2011: Gabriel Spera for *The Rigid Body*
2012: Robin Davidson for *Luminous Other*
2013: J. David Cummings for *Tancho*
2014: Anna George Meek for *The Genome Rhapsodies*
2015: Daneen Wardrop for *Life As* It
2016: Pamela Sutton for *Burning My Birth Certificate*
2017: Michael S. Moos for *The Idea of the Garden*
2018: Barbara Ungar for *Save Our Ship*
2019: Laura Donnelly for *Midwest Gothic*
2020: Peter Grandbois for *Last Night I Aged a Hundred Years*